ME AND MY PONY

The World of Horses

Toni Webber

FRANKLIN WATTS
London · Sydney

© Aladdin Books Ltd 2002

Produced by:
Aladdin Books Ltd
28 Percy Street
London W1T 2BZ

ISBN 0–7496–4491–5

*First published in Great Britain
in 2002 by:*
Franklin Watts
96 Leonard Street
London
EC2A 4XD

Editor:
Harriet Brown

Designers:
Flick, Book Design & Graphics
Simon Morse

Picture researcher:
Brian Hunter Smart

Illustrators:
Peter Barrett, McRae Books – Italy,
David Burroughs, Donald Harley –
BL Kearley, Angus McBride, Simon
Morse, Richard Orr,
Francis Phillipps, Rob Shone,
Stephen Sweet – SGA

Cartoons: Simon Morse

Certain illustrations have
appeared in earlier books
created by Aladdin Books.

Contents

Introduction   3
The horse family   4
Across continents   6
The Western horse   8
Racehorses   10
Riding styles   12
Horses in fiction   14
Horses in history   16
In the beginning   18
Early times   20
Heavy horses   22
The messenger   24
Tack through the ages   26
Working with horses   28
Quiz time   30
Glossary   31
Index   32

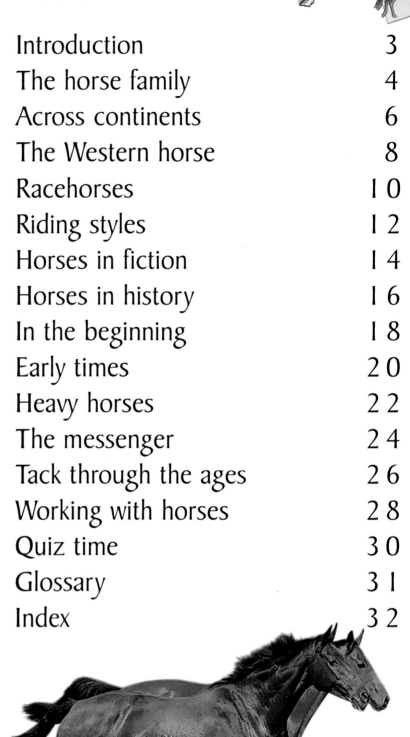

Introduction

The World of Horses is a lively guide to horses from every corner of the globe. Horses have evolved over millions of years to give the creatures that we know and love today. Over the years, horses have had many different uses – from farming to racing, war to delivering messages. In some parts of the world they are still used as work animals but elsewhere they are mainly used in sport and in leisure time.

There is so much to find out about horses. I'll have to write it all in my diary – that should help me to remember!

Did you know?

Look in these boxes for further information about the fascinating world of horses. They contain surprising facts about horses from all over the world.

Q What are these boxes for?

A These question and answer panels are here to help answer your questions about horses. Each panel is relevant to the subject on the rest of the page. Find out how many different breeds there are in the world or how big the first horses were. Learn about mythical horses and find out when stirrups were first invented and why they are so useful.

Monday
I didn't want to go to school today. I was in the middle of re-reading one of my favourite pony books. It's about a girl who owns a horse on a ranch. One day I'm going to go to the Wild West and have my own Western horse!

The horse family

Horses have been used for riding, hauling goods and farm work in many parts of the world. Different types have been bred for different uses. Today, the tiny Shetland pony and the huge work horse look very different, yet they both have a common ancestor.

RUSSIAN GOLDEN HORSE

The narrow Russian horse, the Akhal-Teke, is known as the 'golden horse'. This is because it has a bright, metallic golden sheen on its coat. Originally a desert horse, it is thought to be an ancestor of the Arab. It has great speed and stamina.

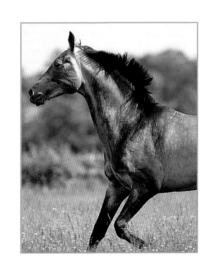

ARAB

Perhaps the most beautiful horse of all time, the Arab is noted for its dished face, glorious head and high tail carriage. It displays amazing stamina and extreme hardiness. It is a native of the Middle East and is used for all types of work, from riding and racing, to pulling carts and carrying produce. The true Arab is not a very big horse. It stands at between only 14.2 and 15 hh (hands high), but it is a unique horse.

Morning
I wish I knew exactly what breed of pony Oscar is. I think he is a New Forest but he doesn't have a pedigree so I can't be sure.

Did you know?

There are about 300 different breeds of horse and pony in the world. They range from the heavy horses of northern Europe to the tiny Falabella pony of South America. One original wild horse, the Tarpan, still exists in captivity. But Przewalski's horse, discovered in Mongolia in the 1920s, is now thought to be extinct. Both of these original wild horses have coarse, heavy heads, a stand-up mane and a dorsal stripe.

HANOVERIAN

Originally bred in Germany, the Hanoverian was used for riding and farmwork. It was later crossed with Thoroughbreds to produce a well-built riding horse. Many leading European riders ride Hanoverians, and these horses are very much in demand for show jumping.

IRISH HUNTER

The Irish hunter is not a breed but a type. Ireland produces some of the finest horses in the world. The Irish draught horse is a strong, well-built working horse. As horses were used less in agriculture, the Irish draught was crossed with the Thoroughbred to produce a riding horse. This was then bred with Connemara horses to become the popular Irish hunter.

Thursday

I am keeping a scrapbook of all the horse breeds of the world – with a difference. I can put a picture of any breed in but only if I have actually seen it. So my book isn't coming along very fast! I told Mum that a tour of Russia would be a good idea, followed by a trip round Scandinavia, but you can guess what she said.

Shetland pony
Scotland

NATIVE PONIES

Of all the regions in the world, the British Isles have the largest number of different breeds of native pony – nine in total. The New Forest and Welsh ponies are ideal for children to ride. Scandinavia and Iceland also have small, hardy native ponies, all of them strong enough to carry grown-ups.

New
Forest
pony
England

Exmoor
pony
England

Q Are horse fairs still held?

A Horse fairs – places where horses and ponies are bought and sold – still exist, such as Golega Fair in Portugal, below. In England, one of the best known is the Stow Fair in Gloucestershire, where young ponies can be bought quite cheaply. The pony breed societies hold annual sales of yearlings that can be trained to become good riding ponies. The sales help control the numbers of wild ponies roaming their natural habitat.

Across continents

Sunday

There are two kinds of pinto horses, the Ovaro and the Tobiano. The Ovaro is dark with patches of white and the Tobiano is white with patches of darker colour. Pintos were popular with native Americans and cowboys.

Today, wherever you go in the world, the main use of horses and ponies is for leisure. In some poor countries the horse still fills its traditional role – that of helping its master to make a living. But, despite this working relationship, the bond between horse and master may still be very close.

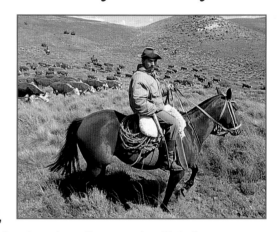

SOUTH AMERICA

This is the home of horses descended from Spanish horses imported nearly 500 years ago. The Argentinians ride Criollos. These are short, stocky horses that are well suited to herding cattle. Criollos are crossed with Thoroughbreds to make very good polo ponies. Argentina is also home to the smallest pony in the world – the Falabella. This tiny pony stands at less than 7 hh.

ASIA

Remains of prehistoric horses have been found in India, and horses are said to have been introduced into China 4,000 years ago. The Chinese pony is very similar to the Mongolian pony, which resembles the early Tarpan horse (page 4).

Waler
Australia

AUSTRALIA

There are no horses native to Australia. The Waler, now an Australian breed, is descended from horses brought by settlers in the 18th century. Brumbies, feral horses living in the outback, come from horses turned loose in the gold rushes of the 19th century.

CONQUISTADORS

The Spanish who discovered and conquered the New World, the conquistadors, brought their horses with them. These caused as much interest, awe and excitement among the native Americans as did the arrival of the white men themselves. Until this time, the American continent had no horses at all. Some escaped into the wild, and were the ancestors of the feral horses of the plains.

Appaloosa
USA

Pinto
USA

NORTH AMERICAN HORSES

The American Quarter Horse (left), with its short bursts of speed and ability to turn and twist, is ideally suited to cattle-herding. The remarkable Tennessee Walking Horse, with its amazingly comfortable running gait, suited the plantation owner's need to spend all day in the saddle without getting tired.

Tennessee Walking Horse
USA

MUSTANGS

The wild horse of America, the mustang, is a direct descendant of the horses that came over with the Spanish conquistadors. Big herds of these feral horses used to roam the plains of the central USA but they were long considered worthless. So, fifty years ago, a registry of Spanish mustang horses was established with the aim of preserving their best characteristics – hardiness, intelligence and stamina.

The Western horse

In the American West, the horse had a particular function – herding cattle across the vast plains of the continent and carrying its rider many kilometres a day. It is no wonder that the Western horse displays special characteristics and wears a saddle and bridle well suited to its role in life.

Later – I'm in big trouble. I took Oscar's noseband off to turn him into a cowboy horse and now I've lost it. I was sure I'd left it in the tack room. So now I've got to use my pocket money to buy a new one. Still, he really looked like a Western horse!

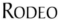

RODEO

Rodeo competitions provided cowboys with a chance to show off their riding and cattle skills. Today, they are a popular attraction in America. They offer prizes to riders who can stay on a bucking horse the longest, rope a calf the quickest and sit on a bull without falling off.

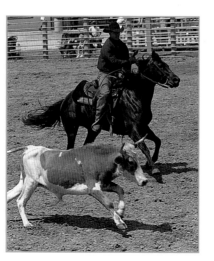

JUNIOR RODEO RIDERS

America has an association of young rodeo riders. Their ages range from eight to 19 years and they compete at all sorts of cowboy contests. Rodeos include goat tying, calf roping, steer wrestling and riding, bareback riding and bronco riding.

cantle horn pommel

seat

fender

ties

stirrup

WESTERN SADDLE AND BRIDLE

The seat of the Western saddle is deep for the comfort of the rider on a long ride. The horn is for attaching a rope when roping steers. The cantle and pommel are high to 'lock' the rider in position when twisting and turning during the process of herding cattle. The Western bridle has long shanks on the bit that are used in conjunction with a leather curb strap to act on the horse's poll (the part of the head between the ears). Western bridles don't have a noseband. Split reins – reins not buckled together – are popular. One-handed riding is normal, so cowboys steer their horses using neck-reining.

MYTHS AND MODERN WAYS

Cowboys did spend many hours in the saddle and they slept under the stars. But they did not ride the huge horses that you see in Western films. Real cowboys preferred small horses, often ponies, and usually rode more than one a day. Cowboys sometimes changed mounts six times a day. Today, cowboys are more likely to be seen on quad bikes or at rodeos than out on a horse.

Annabel and I tried roping a fence post and the loop never came near enough. Just imagine trying it with a moving steer!

WESTERN TRAILS

The modern-day rider can enjoy a great holiday at a Western ranch catering for tourists, riding out on the old cowboy trails. Trail rides can be just one day or you can go on longer rides lasting several days. Accommodation usually involves camping out at night and cooking your own food on an open fire. Trail riding is enjoyed by many people.

Racehorses

From the time when horses were first domesticated, riders have tried to outdo each other. Racing has existed as an organised sport for about 400 years. Today it is worldwide. The best horses are greatly admired and can be worth huge amounts of money.

THOROUGHBRED

The Thoroughbred is the fastest horse in the world. It is descended from one of three Arab stallions, the Darley Arabian, the Byerley Turk and the Godolphin Barb. Every racehorse entered in the General Stud Book has at least one in its pedigree. The Thoroughbred develops early, which is why two-year-olds can be ridden and raced. Every Thoroughbred's official birthday is January 1st.

WHERE IT ALL BEGAN

The ancient Greeks enjoyed public racing, but in much of Europe for the next thousand years or so, any racing was mainly private. In the late 17th century, it became more formalised in England, and other countries soon followed suit. The Jockey Club was created to oversee the sport.

STEEPLECHASING

Racing over jumps used to be held between two landmarks, often the steeples of churches (hence steeplechasing). The world's most famous race over jumps – the Grand National – began in 1839. Most horses in jump racing today start by racing on the flat. If they are too slow for flat racing, they are tried over hurdles, then over jumps. If the longer distance suits them they can race for many more years.

RACING AROUND THE WORLD

There are several great races. Among the most famous are the English Derby, the American Kentucky Derby, the Australian Melbourne Cup and the French Prix de l'Arc de Triomphe. Race meetings are held all over the world and provide a focal point for the local population. Hong Kong's racecourse, Happy Valley, is set in the middle of the crowded city.

The English Derby, run at Epsom
England

Happy Valley Racecourse
Hong Kong

The Kentucky Derby, Churchill Downs
USA

Friday
I think I would quite like to be a jockey. Girls and boys can be apprenticed to racehorse trainers nowadays. But Dad says it's a hard life and only the very best can get to the top. Perhaps I could be the first girl to win the English Derby!

TROTTERS

Harness-racing is popular in America and France. The horses have been trained to move at an amazingly swift trot instead of a gallop. Their other artificial gait, the pace, is where the legs on the same side move forward at the same time. These two gaits ensure the horse pulls the two-wheeled, lightweight sulky very smoothly.

11

Riding styles

Through the ages, most riding styles have changed. A few have stayed much the same as always. Others have been affected by clothing styles, social attitudes or improvements in technique. In some cases, the interest of modern-day enthusiasts keeps an older riding style going.

3 pm – I tried riding like a mediaeval knight on Oscar the other day. They used to ride with really long stirrups. It wasn't very easy, especially when it came to rising trot. It's almost impossible to stand up in the stirrups when your legs are straight to start with!

RACING

An American jockey called Tod Sloan changed the style of race-riding forever in the 19th century. Before he came to England to ride in races, jockeys rode with long stirrups. Tod introduced the very short stirrup leather. He was laughed at and called a "monkey on a stick". Despite this, his technique was soon copied by jockeys everywhere.

Did you know?

The Spanish Riding School in Vienna trains its horses in what is called the classic style of horsemanship. The beautiful white Lipizzaner stallions are taught High School movements (right). The Spanish Riding School travels all over the world giving demonstrations, which are well worth a visit. The horses are very supple, calm and obedient, and wonderfully in tune with their talented riders.

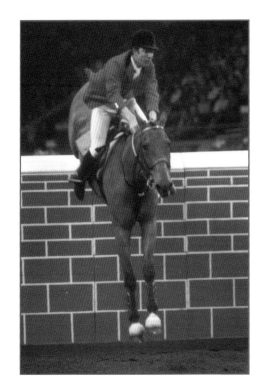

JUMPING

Everyone today is taught the forward seat when jumping. This lets the hands follow the movement of the horse and keeps the rider's weight evenly distributed. This method is one hundred years old. It dates back to the teachings of an Italian cavalry officer, Federico Caprilli. Before that, riders leant forward on take-off and back on landing.

WESTERN

With a deep seat and straight legs, cowboys found that they could ride for many kilometres and not get too tired. Provided the saddle fits properly, this style is kind to the horse, too. Western horses are trained to respond to the reins touching the neck. A touch on the right side makes the horse turn left and vice versa.

SIDE-SADDLE

Side-saddle riding is considered a very elegant riding style. In the past it was the only acceptable way for a lady to ride. The 'leaping head', the down-turned horn fitted below the upward horn on the saddle, makes it possible for side saddle riders to have a firm seat, jump and gallop safely.

MEDIAEVAL KNIGHTS

Cavalry was an important part of the army and all officers were mounted. They rode with long stirrups, straight legs and their feet forwards. This style looks similar to that of Western riders. The armour worn by the military horsemen of Northern Europe was so bulky that only very strong horses could carry them. Some needed cranes to lift them onto their horses. If a soldier fell off, he would never be able to get on again.

13

Horses in fiction

Tuesday
Before I had Oscar, I spent
most of my time reading.
I think I've read all the
horse books ever written!
But Oscar takes up so
much of my day, reading
has moved into second
place. Now, most of my
books are practical ones
on pony care.

Stories about horses have been popular for many years, from the classics of earlier days to the pony books of today. Some fictional horses live forever, continuing to delight each generation of readers. Some of them are listed here.

SILVER

This horse was almost certainly the first to become famous through radio and television. He is a handsome grey who belongs to the Lone Ranger. The Lone Ranger is a masked man who rides anonymously through the Wild West, solving crimes and restoring law and order wherever he goes.

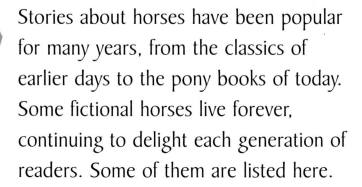

FLICKA

Flicka is the horse heroine of 'My Friend Flicka', a book written by Mary O'Hara about the love of a boy for his horse. The setting is a ranch in Wyoming and the book gives a vivid picture of domesticating and training wild horses in the West just before the Second World War. The book is beautifully written and well worth reading. No longer in print, it can be found in second-hand bookshops.

BLACK BEAUTY

A young writer, Anna Sewell, hated seeing carriage horses in bearing reins. These are straps that forced horses to carry their heads at an uncomfortable angle. She wrote a book about the life of a carriage horse, Black Beauty. She included other characters, such as Merrylegs and Ginger. The book is a classic and led to bearing reins being outlawed in the UK.

Afternoon – Annabel and I both belong to our local library, but we can't always find the books we want to read. So Annabel said why don't we get together with friends at the stables and form our own book-lending group. I thought that was a brilliant idea. So that's what we've done. There are loads of books I haven't read yet.

THE RED PONY

'The Red Pony' is a short story by the American author John Steinbeck. The Red Pony is a lovable little pony, which is adored by its owner, a young boy. The pony falls ill and dies and the boy blames his father for the pony's death. The story describes how the two of them struggle to build a new relationship. The story, which does finally have a happy ending, was made into a prize-winning film in 1949.

ROSINANTE

This horse is an example of beauty being in the eye of the beholder. Rosinante is an ugly old nag, who generally fails in anything he is asked to do. But to his owner, Don Quixote, a self-styled knight, he is a status symbol and the best horse in the world. 'Don Quixote de la Mancha' was written by Miguel de Cervantes in the 17th century and is a classic of European literature.

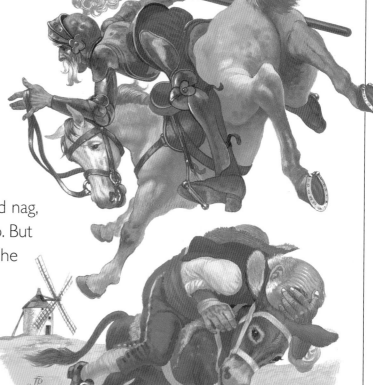

Horses in history

Just as there are famous people in history, so there are some horses whose names will never be forgotten. A few are remembered because their owners were great men, but others – mostly racehorses – are legends in their own right.

Saturday
What do you think Oscar would have to do to go down in history? He's certainly not a charger or a racehorse. But he's a really cool pony and I'm lucky to have him. He's going down in my history, anyway.

BUCEPHALUS

Bucephalus belonged to Alexander the Great. He was thought to be unrideable until Alexander realised that the horse was frightened of his own shadow. By turning Bucephalus towards the sun, Alexander could mount him. Alexander became a powerful warrior and rode Bucephalus in all his campaigns.

WELLINGTON

COPENHAGEN

Copenhagen, a chestnut, was a grandson of the racehorse Eclipse. He was much loved by his owner, the Duke of Wellington. He accompanied the 'Iron Duke' through many of his battles, including the victory over Napoleon at Waterloo.

CHALK HORSES

Figures of horses have been carved into the chalk downland of Southern England for thousands of years. The oldest chalk horse is at Uffington, Oxfordshire, and is thought to be 3,000 years old. A new one may be carved in Kent, near the entrance to the Channel Tunnel between England and France.

ECLIPSE

Possibly the greatest racehorse that has ever lived, Eclipse was born in 1764 during an eclipse of the sun. He never lost a race. His owner once predicted the result of a race as "Eclipse first and the rest nowhere". A chestnut horse, Eclipse sired (fathered) 335 winners after finishing his racing career. He died, aged 25, in 1789.

RED RUM

Red Rum won the Grand National, one of the hardest steeplechases in the world, no fewer than three times. His first win, in 1973, broke the course record. He completed the four-and-a-half mile course, over 30 jumps, in 9 minutes 1.9 seconds.

I'm making a scrapbook about Oscar and me. I'll keep a record of everything we do together and call it 'The History of Oscar'.

SECRETARIAT

In 1970, Secretariat, one of the most famous American racehorses, was born in Virginia. In his career, he won the USA's Triple Crown – the Kentucky Derby, the Belmont Stakes and the Preakness Stakes. He completed the Kentucky Derby in the fastest time ever and won the Belmont Stakes by 31 lengths, an incredible achievement.

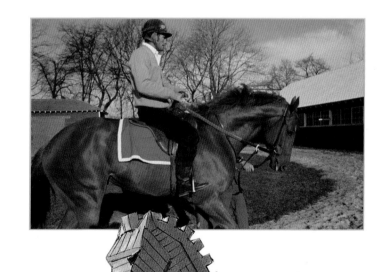

Q When is a horse not a horse?

A Apart from a clothes horse, the answer is the Trojan Horse. In Greek mythology, the Greeks were besieging the city of Troy but could not break the Trojans' resistance. Then they built a huge wooden horse, in which they hid dozens of warriors. They gave it to the Trojans as a gift, which the Trojans accepted. Once inside the city, the warriors poured out of the horse and captured Troy.

In the beginning

Early horses looked nothing like the horses of today. It took 50 million years of evolution for the cat-sized creature that lived in the Northern Hemisphere to become the handsome, elegant horse we all admire now. Only in the last 5,000 years has the horse been ridden by man.

HYRACOTHERIUM

Also known as Eohippus ('Dawn Horse'), Hyracotherium was a funny little creature. It had four toes on its front feet and three toes on the back. From all the fossilised bones found in the southern USA, it seems likely that it originated on the American continent.

Hyracotherium

MESOHIPPUS

The next stage in the evolution was the Mesohippus. It had a similar bone structure to the Hyracotherium, but was bigger. Still a small creature, it was beginning to emerge from the forest to graze on the plains. Its feet were still multi-toed, but the outer toes were less pronounced. Its weight was carried on the central toe.

Mesohippus

INTO DANGER

The little prehistoric horses, coming out of the safety of the forest, were able to run quite fast. This was their way of avoiding danger. But they were no match for predatory birds. These creatures, with their sharp eyesight, could easily spot the tiny horses, in spite of their striped camouflage. Many horses ended up as a tasty morsel.

Q How big were the first horses?

A They were very small. Hyracotherium was not much bigger than a domestic cat. Certainly too small for a human to ride, even if early man had been in existence at the time. Throughout the millions of years of evolution, horses got bigger and stronger.

HOT-BLOODS AND COLD-BLOODS

As the horse evolved, two types emerged. In the northern countries, the cold-bloods were predominant. They developed into the heavy horses of today, powerfully built, strong creatures. They could be trained to pull a plough or wagon or to carry a man in a full suit of armour. Further south were the hot-bloods, horses like the desert Arab. These were lighter in build but very hardy and tough. Many of today's horses are crosses between the two types and are known as warm-bloods.

EQUUS

This is the true horse, common ancestor of all our present-day horses. It was a single-toed mammal standing about 13 hh. Equus had a large head, heavy neck, faint stripes on its fore and hindquarters and possibly a dorsal stripe along its backbone. Its mane was short and stood up like a shaving brush.

Merichippus

Equus

MERICHIPPUS

Merichippus was more recognisable as a horse. The outer toes had almost disappeared and the central toe was broadening into a hoof. This was a creature of the plains, no longer feeding on trees but capable of eating grass. Its natural defence was to run away. In spite of the vast prairies of America, horses disappeared from the American continent. They did not return for several thousand years, until brought back by the conquistadors in the 16th century.

Morning
I had a nightmare last night. I dreamed that I was a Dawn Horse living in a prehistoric world. I was being chased by a caveman. I was so glad to wake up!

Early times

Most of the great horse people of the olden days, between 2000 and 1000 BC, lived in or roamed the Middle East. Some used horses for riding or as pack animals; others harnessed them to chariots. Either way, the horse was a symbol indicating a great chieftain or warrior.

Hun

SCYTHIANS

These people flourished in the Altai mountains of Central Asia around 1500 BC. The frozen tombs of Scythian chieftains and their horses were discovered in the 1920s. They revealed that the horses were fed on grain and that their tack consisted of lavishly decorated felt saddle pads. The bridles were crowned by reindeer head-dresses.

EASTERN HORSEMEN

Most tribes of Central Asia were nomadic, moving about in pursuit of food supplies. The tribesmen were superb horsemen. The Huns were so dedicated to their steeds that they dismounted only to sleep. The Chinese fought and traded with the Huns. They also found that horses flourished in the damp lowlands of China, so they established vast breeding centres.

EGYPTIANS

The Egyptians are believed to have adapted the use of horses when they were introduced into Egypt by the nomadic Hyksos tribe. They drew two-wheeled chariots and were almost certainly used by the Egyptian army. Other peoples of the Near East and North Africa were excellent horsemen, including the Babylonians and Assyrians.

ROMANS

Roman armies generally fought on foot but Roman generals, wishing to make an impression, would enter a captured town or city on horseback. Horses were also used in chariots for racing and parade in ceremonies. It was in the later part of the Roman Empire that the cavalry came into widespread use.

GREEKS

Greek horsemanship is well known because of the literature that has survived from ancient times. Best known of the ancient Greek equine writers is Xenophon. He was a general who wrote in detail describing the way horses should be trained and cared for. Many of his ideas are still valid today although saddles and stirrups had not been invented – the Greeks always rode bareback.

Q What about mythical horses?

A Best known of legendary horses is Pegasus, the winged horse of Greek mythology. He is said to have sprung from the blood of Medusa and was caught with the help of a magic bridle made of gold. His rider, Bellerophon, tried to take Pegasus to heaven. But this angered Zeus, the chief of the gods, and he sent a fly to sting Pegasus. Bellerophon fell to earth but Pegasus flew on and became a constellation in the night sky. Another mythical creature was the centaur, half man, half horse. The centaur Chiron survives in the sky as the constellation Sagittarius.

Afternoon – I'm glad we live in the 21st century. I wouldn't have wanted to ride without stirrups all the time like they did in ancient times. Annabel and I tried riding without stirrups for an hour and it was so tiring. It's amazing how much support you get from them. I couldn't wait for the ride to end.

Saturday
There is a farm near us that gives brewery horses a holiday and also breeds Shire foals. It is lovely to see them in the summer, cantering about and enjoying themselves in the sunshine. Oscar's not much bigger than the foals!

Heavy horses

In their time, the size and strength of heavy horses made them the most important of the horse breeds, and even today they are impressive. But in many places they no longer have a role, and only careful conservation will prevent them from dying out.

OLD AMERICAN HORSES

The most versatile all-purpose horse in America is the Morgan. It is a combination of the best qualities of both draught and riding horses – powerful, intelligent and with great stamina.

PLOUGHING WITH HORSES

Until 50 years ago, heavy horses were used for farm work throughout the Western world. They are still used in some countries. These massive but willing animals were the engines of agriculture. They can pull ploughs and threshing machines and work tirelessly all day.

JOUSTING

A man in full armour is very heavy and the horse had to be immensely strong to carry him. During the Age of Chivalry, tournaments became popular. Knights competed against each other, trying to knock each other off their horses. The two riders used their lances as battering rams.

TODAY'S CAVALRY

Heavy horses are no longer used by the cavalry, which does not need weight-carriers to take soldiers, even in ceremonial dress. The cavalry has no role in modern warfare but it is still an impressive sight when taking part in state ceremonies. The annual Trooping of the Colour on Horseguards Parade in London is a spectacular sight.

DRAY HORSES

In Britain, several big breweries still use heavy horses to pull their drays. It is not unusual to see beer barrels being unloaded outside a public house, while the pair of Shire horses harnessed to the dray enjoy their lunch

from nosebags. Classes for tradesmen's drays are usually held at agricultural shows. They parade around the arena giving a magnificent display.

Suffolk Punch
England

Clydesdale
Scotland

Dutch Draught
Holland

HEAVY HORSES TODAY

Efforts are being made to conserve breeds that might otherwise die out. The Suffolk Punch, a British breed that is always chestnut and has no feather (long hair) on its legs, is the most endangered. Special societies support the preservation of working breeds around the world.

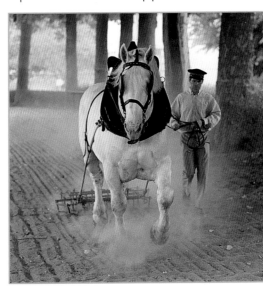

The messenger

The speed and stamina of the horse made it the perfect method of carrying messages, and for many centuries, they served as the fastest messengers. From 5th century Persia, through 13th century Mongolia, to 19th century America, horses, ridden in shifts, were the main means of taking news across the world.

Mum has made me two saddle bags, so that Annabel and I can take something to eat when we go off on a long ride.

THE PONY EXPRESS

The Pony Express was a rapid postal service between the central USA and California. In 1860, a private company established 190 stations along the 3,220-kilometre route between St Joseph, Missouri, and Sacramento, California. They bought 500 fast horses and recruited 120 riders to carry the saddle bags of messages across the Great Plains, over two towering mountain ranges and through the vast badlands of Utah and Nevada. The first relay arrived in just over 10 days, and later deliveries were made in only seven.

Sacramento
Salt Lake City
St Joseph
St Louis

THE AMERICAN STAGECOACH

In the American west in the late 19th century, horse-drawn stage coaches travelled between widely separated towns, carrying valuable cargo and passengers. Bands of outlaws often waylaid a stage coach, taking its strongbox and robbing passengers. Sheriffs deputised local residents as a 'posse' to pursue thieves on horseback.

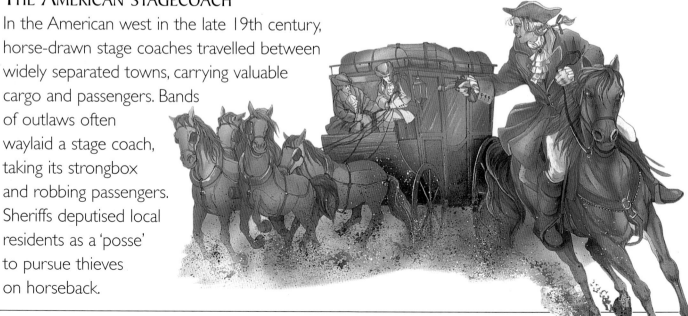

PAUL REVERE

Paul Revere was one of several horsemen who slipped out of Boston on the night of 18 April, 1775, to warn outlying towns that British troops were on the march against the Massachusetts colonists. The next morning, the British met strong resistance at Lexington and Concord in battles that marked the beginning of the American Revolution.

DELIVERING NEWS

Most long distance riders use relays of horses to cover great distances in a short time. The Mongol Post in the 13th century routinely travelled 200 km in one day. The fastest

ride they recorded was 341 km in one day. In the Middle Ages, heralds (above) used to relay important news to their king. These knights had distinct coats of arms that were used to identify them in battle.

ROYAL MAIL COACHES

The Royal Mail coaches carried the post from London to different places in the British Isles. The coaches were usually pulled by four horses, which would be changed at regular intervals. The great boast of the coach drivers was that they would always get through, no matter what snowstorms or other terrible conditions they came across on the way, and that they were always on schedule. Passengers could also travel on the coaches.

Thursday
It must have been exciting to be a Pony Express rider, except that the journey was dangerous and scary. But taking the post and dashing off into hostile country must have been fantastic. No wonder there were so many riders willing to tackle it.

Tack through the ages

Various methods of controlling the horse have been tried since ancient times. Some of them aren't very different from those used today. Saddles were a later development than bits, but it was the invention of the stirrup that transformed riding. Stirrups gave riders the chance to acquire a balanced seat and to ride in harmony with their horse.

11 am – I can't imagine using a bridle without a bit. Mind you, my instructor at the stables says that in the right hands a bitless bridle is just as effective as a snaffle bridle. I don't think Oscar would mind what I use – he thinks he looks gorgeous in anything.

THE BITLESS BRIDLE

The hackamore, or bitless, bridle is widely used but always with care. It acts on the nose and, in rough hands, can easily cut off a horse's air supply. The cowboys of South America, the gauchos, usually use a form of bitless bridle, knotted under the chin. They often use a single rein, but their horsemanship is superb.

EARLY BITS

The snaffle bit was first used by Iron-Age Celts, originally as a straight-bar and then with a joint. The early jointed snaffle was almost exactly the same as the snaffle bit of today. Snaffle bits act on the tongue and the corners of the horse's mouth and cause it to raise its head.

Celtic snaffle bit

Modern snaffle bit

shank

Mediaeval
curb bit

THE MIDDLE AGES

In the Middle Ages bits were very elaborate. The shanks were decorated and usually very long. The mouthpiece had a high central port, or hump. When pressure was applied to the reins, the bit acted on both the bars and roof of the mouth. This caused the horse to bend heavily at its poll. Knights preferred to use curb bits.

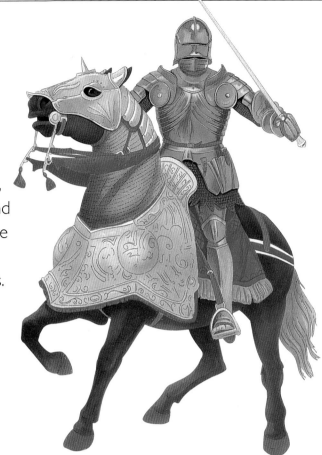

HOW A MODERN CURB WORKS

The modern curb bit works in exactly the same way as the mediaeval curb. But the modern shanks are shorter and the mouthpiece is less severe. Pressure on the lower rein causes the bit to press on the bars of the mouth. It causes the curb chain to tighten in the chin groove and the headpiece to press on the poll. Instinctively the horse will lower its head, bend at the poll and flex its jaw. The curb bit can be combined with a snaffle bit to form a double bridle.

Q When were stirrups invented?

A Stirrups were developed by the Huns in the 5th century AD. They first learned to make a saddle with a tree (frame) and then attached stirrups to the framework of the saddle. The Huns were archers and galloped alongside their enemies, shooting at them over their shoulders. Stirrups let them do this without losing their balance. Modern-day mounted games players rely on stirrups for balance in the same way.

Roman
saddle

27

Working with horses

If you love riding and horses, it is not surprising that you would like to go on being with horses. You may choose to go on riding in your leisure time, at weekends or in the holidays. Or you may, like many others before you, decide to work with horses full time.

TEACHING

Firstly, you need to be a proficient rider. Secondly, it's important that you enjoy people as well as horses. Today, instructors have formal qualifications and you should become qualified if you want to teach. The British Horse Society (BHS) has a course of examinations that you can take to become a riding instructor.

Did you know?

Veterinary courses are some of the hardest to get on to. Qualifying as a vet takes longer than becoming a doctor. You will need good exam grades, usually in chemistry, biology and physics or maths, to be accepted by a veterinary college. Once qualified, you can specialise in equine medicine. Another option would be to train as a veterinary nurse. Alternatively, farriery and saddlery are equestrian careers that offer great job satisfaction.

Afternoon – Oscar really enjoys lots of company, especially with people. I think he would like to have a job where he could be with humans. He would work on his laptop when he was travelling on the train to his office each day. Imagine that?!

GROOM

A groom's job can be very rewarding if you work with a leading rider in the eventing or show jumping world. The British Horse Society awards a groom's diploma to those who pass the appropriate exams.

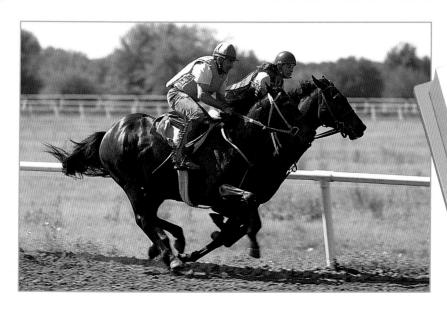

RACING

Jockeys start as apprentices and may work in a racing stable for a year or more before riding in races. To get a place, you can apply directly to a trainer or to the Jockey Club to get on a training scheme. Or you may be taken on as a stable lad (even if you are a girl!), eventually becoming Head Lad. For top jockeys, the rewards can be very great.

Tuesday
I think it would be good fun to be a jockey and travel all over the country riding in races. When you start as a jockey you can claim a weight allowance. This means that your horse carries less weight than the others. The amount you can claim reduces as you win more races. Eventually you can't claim any reduction at all.

RUNNING YOUR OWN STABLES

If you have – or can buy – a stable complex with land attached, you could run a livery business. You don't need any particular qualifications for this, although some universities and colleges offer a degree or diploma course in equine business studies. If you want to provide a full livery service, it helps if you have stable management qualifications.

Q What about Riding for the Disabled?

A Riding for the Disabled is not really a career option because people who work with disabled riders are all volunteers. Nevertheless, the job is both worthwhile and rewarding, although it can be physically quite hard. Much depends on the disability of the riders and how much support and assistance they need. Most areas have Riding for the Disabled groups which meet regularly. They always need volunteers. Everyone will tell you how beneficial riding can be, as the riders gain confidence from being with ponies.

Quiz time

How much do you know about the world of horses? Here is a chance for you and your friends to test your knowledge.

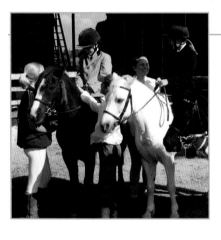

3 Name two of the contests in a young riders' rodeo.

4 Who was the first jockey to ride with very short stirrups?

5 Where would you find the Spanish riding school?

6 Who wrote 'Black Beauty'?

7 What was the name of the Duke of Wellington's horse?

8 How many toes did the 'dawn horse' (hyracotherium or eohippus) have on its front feet and how many on the back?

9 Which heavy horse comes from Scotland?

10 What are the people who look after racehorses in a racing stable known as?

1 Where do the 'golden' horses come from?

2 What name is given to the wild horses of North America?

Useful addresses

The Pony Club
The Pony Club HQ
NAC
Stoneleigh Park
Kenilworth
Warwickshire
CV8 2RW
Tel: 01327 361 388
www.pony-club.org.uk

The British Horse Society
Stoneleigh Deer Park,
Kenilworth
Warwickshire
CV8 2XZ
Tel: 08701 202 244
Fax: 01926 707 800
www.bhs.org.uk

11 am – Annabel and I went in for a quiz on Saturday. Some of the questions were on the history of horses and we got every one right. Cool!

Answers

1 Russia 2 Mustangs 3 Bronco riding, bareback riding, calf roping, steer wrestling and goat tying 4 Tod Sloan 5 Vienna, Austria 6 Anna Sewell 7 Copenhagen 8 Four on the front, three on the back 9 Clydesdale 10 Stable lads

Glossary

bit
A metal bar attached to the reins that fits in the pony's mouth.

chalk horse
A horse shape that is carved into the side of a chalk hill.

cowboy
A person on horseback who drives cattle many miles across vast plains.

dorsal stripe
A stripe of dark hair that runs along the back of a horse from the mane to the tail.

dray
A heavy cart that is pulled by horses. Drays are used to carry barrels of beer in the UK.

feral horses
Horses that are untamed and live in the wild.

gaucho
A South American cowboy.

groom
A person who looks after a horse.

hackamore
A bridle that has no bit. The horse is controlled by pressure exerted on the nose of the horse.

hands
Horses and ponies are measured in hands. It is a unit of measurement that is roughly the width of an adult's hand. One hand is equal to 10 cm.

jousting
A tournament in the Middle Ages where knights fought with lances.

lance
A long pole that was carried by knights in jousting competitions. It was used for knocking the opponent off the horse.

livery
The name given to the practice of keeping a pony at stables that aren't your own. You pay a fee to the owner of the stables.

mustang
A wild horse of North America.

neck-reining
Guiding a horse with only one hand on the reins.

pacer
Horse with an artificial gait, in which both legs on one side move forward at the same time.

rodeo
A competition in which cowboys display their riding and cattle-roping skills.

steeplechasing
A horse race that is run over jumps.

steer
A young bull or ox, which is often used in rodeo competitions.

sulky
A two-wheeled, lightweight cart used in harness-racing.

trail riding
Exploring open countryside on horseback.

yearling
A horse that is between one and two years old.

Index

agriculture 5, 22

bearing reins 15
bit 26, 27, 31
Black Beauty 15, 30
books 14-15
breed 4, 5, 6, 7, 22, 23
bridle 26, 27
British Horse Society 28
brumbies 6
Bucephalus 16

cavalry 23
centaur 21
chalk horses 16, 31
chariot 20, 21
coaches 25
conquistadors 7, 19
Copenhagen 16, 30
cowboys 9, 13, 26, 31

dorsal stripe 4, 19, 31
draught horse 5, 22, 23
dray horses 23

Eclipse 16, 17
Egyptians 20
Equus 19
evolution 18

feral horses 6, 7, 31
Flicka 14

gaucho 26, 31
Greeks 10, 17, 21
groom 28, 31

hackamore 26, 31
Happy Valley 11
heavy horses 4, 19, 22-23
heralds 25
horse fairs 5
Huns 20, 27
Hyracotherium 18, 30

Irish hunter 5

jockey 10, 11, 12, 29, 30
jousting 22, 31
jumping 13

knight 12, 13, 15, 22, 25, 27, 31

lance 22, 31
legend 16, 21
livery 29, 31

Merichippus 19
Mesohippus 18
mustangs 7, 30, 31

native ponies 5

pace 11, 31
Pony Express 24, 25
prehistoric horses 6, 18, 19
Przewalski's Horse 4
racehorses 10-11, 16, 17, 30

racing 3, 4, 10, 11, 12, 17, 21, 29
'Red Pony' 15
Red Rum 17
Riding for the Disabled 29
riding stlyes 12-13
rodeo 8, 9, 30, 31
Romans 21
Rosinante 15

saddle 7, 8, 12, 20, 21, 26, 27
  side-saddle 13
  Western 9
Scythians 20
Secretariat 17
show jumping 5, 28
Silver 14
Spanish riding school 12, 30
stagecoach 24
steeplechasing 10, 17, 31
stirrups 12, 13, 21, 26, 27, 30
sulky 11, 31

tack 20, 26-27
Tarpan 4, 6
teaching 28
Thoroughbred 5, 6, 10
trail riding 9, 31
Trojan horse 17

vet 28

Welsh pony 5
Western bridle 9
Western horse 8-9
Western riding 13, 14
wild horses 4, 5, 6, 7, 14, 30, 31

Photo credits

Abbreviations: l-left, r-right, b-bottom, t-top, c-centre, m-middle

Front cover, 1, 3b, 7ml, 9ml, 13tl, 13c, 21ml, 22c, 25tr, 30c, 31 both — Corel. Back cover, 5ml, 9tr, 16br, 23tl, 28br, 29ml, 30ml — Select Pictures. 2b, 4tr, 5tl, 5mt, 8bm, 9br, 10tl, 12c, 23ml, 23br, 27 both, 29tl, 29br — Horsepix. 4c, 5br, 6 both, 7mr, 10c, 10br, 11tl, 11br, 12br, 13bl, 17ml, 19tl, 25c, 28ml — Kit Houghton Photography. 11ct — Kelly-Mooney Photography/CORBIS. 11ml — Jerry Cooke/CORBIS. 12tr — Leonard de Selva/CORBIS. 14-15 all — The Kobal Collection. 16c — Brian Hunter Smart. 17tr, 17mr — Bettmann/CORBIS. 22mr — Corbis Royalty Free. 25tr — Photodisc.